D0878277

Oregon Bucket List Adventure Guide & Journal

Explore 50 Natural Wonders You Must See & Log Your Experience!

Bridge Press

East Meadow Public Library
1886 Front Street, East Meadow, NY 11554
www.eastmeadow.info
(516) 794-2570

1

Bridge Press
dp@purplelink.org

Please consider writing a review!
Just visit: purplelink.org/review

ISBN: 978-1-955149-16-7

FREE BONUS

Find Out 31 Incredible Places You Can Visit Next! Just Go To:

purplelink.org/travel

Table of Contents

How to Use This Book

Welcome to your very own adventure guide to exploring the natural wonders of the state of Oregon. Not only does this book lay out the most wonderful places to visit and sights to see in the vast state, but it also serves as a journal so you can record your own experiences.

Adventure Guide

Sorted by region, this guide offers 50 amazing wonders of nature found in Oregon for you to go see and explore. These can be visited in any order, and this book will help keep track of where you've been and where to look forward to going next.

Each portion describes the area or place, what to look for, how to get there, and what you may need to bring along. A map is also included so you can map out your destinations.

Journal Your Experience

Following each location description is a fillable journal page for you. During or after your visit, you can jot down significant sights encountered, events confronted, people involved, and memories you gained while on your adventure in the journal section. This will add even more value to your experience and keep record of your time spent witnessing the greatest wonders of Oregon.

GPS Coordinates and Codes

As you can imagine, not all of the locations in this book have a physical address. Fortunately, some of our listed wonders are either located within a National Park or Reserve, or are near a city, town, or place of business. For those that are not associated with a specific location, it is easiest to map it using GPS coordinates.

Luckily, Google has a system of codes that converts the coordinates into pin drop locations that Google Maps is able to interpret and navigate.

Each adventure in this guide will include both the GPS coordinates along with general directions on how to find the location, and Google Plus codes whenever possible.

How to find a location using Google Plus:

1. Open Google Maps on your device.
2. In the search bar, type the Google Plus code as it is printed on the page.
3. Once the pin is located, you can tap on "Directions" for step-by-step navigation.

It is important that you are prepared for poor cell signals. It is recommended to route your location and ensure that the directions are accessible offline. Depending on your device and the distance of some locations, you may need to travel with a backup battery source.

About Oregon

The Oregon Trail might be the first to come to mind when thinking about this part of the Pacific Northwest, but the first European traders and settlers to explore what is now Oregon landed in the mid-1500s. These were mostly Spanish sailors sent northeast from the Philippines across the Pacific Ocean and many of their ships wrecked on the Oregon Coast. The indigenous tribes who called the land home met similar fates as they did in other parts of the country, as they were forcibly relocated to reservations, especially when Oregon became a U.S. territory in 1848.

Today, Oregon is known for its large cities like Portland. These cities are known for their thriving music scene, as well as their food and drink, as Portland has the largest number of breweries of any city in the world. Tourism makes up a large portion of the state's income, and while Portland is often a center for those visiting this state, Oregon's many natural wonders draw climbers, hikers, rafters, kayakers, and nature enthusiasts from all over the world. Its often remote natural beauty also attracts filmmakers; movies filmed in Oregon include *The Goonies*, *One Flew Over the Cuckoo's Nest*, and *Stand By Me*.

Landscape and Climate

Oregon is bordered by the Columbia River on its north side, which separates it from Washington State, as well as the Snake River on its east side, which separates it from Idaho. Oregon's landscape and climate have been affected universally by its volcanic activity, which has formed canyons, lava flows, and even dry deserts.

The Oregon Coast stretches for 362 miles along Oregon's western edge, bordered by the vast Pacific Ocean and the Oregon Coast

Mountain Range. The Oregon Coast National Wildlife Refuge Complex covers 320 of the 362 miles and protects the various species that call the coast home. As the Oregon Coast has some of the most diverse marine ecology in the world, that's quite a few species! Several species of seals make their home on the Oregon Coast, and gray whales, humpback whales, and orcas migrate past Oregon every year on their way to the Arctic. Birders also prize this part of Oregon for its seabirds, shorebirds, and even birds of prey like bald eagles and ospreys.

The Oregon High Desert is located in the central and southeast parts of Oregon, east of the Cascade Mountain Range and south of the Blue Mountains. Technically, much of the High Desert only qualifies as scrubland or steppe, but it still only averages 15 millimeters a year of rainfall. Steens Mountain is the highest point, at 9,733 feet above sea level, but the High Desert averages about 4,000 feet above sea level, giving the region its name. The vegetation that grows in the desert includes many of Oregon's native wildflowers, and the High Desert contains the oldest known tree in Oregon, a juniper tree which is estimated to be 1,600 years old. Hundreds of animal species can be found in the High Desert, everything from small mammals to birds of prey to bighorn sheep.

Oregon's Forest might be the first on your mind when considering Oregon's natural beauty, but it's a little more spread out than the coast and the desert. Densely forested areas concentrate in Willamette Valley, which contains the big metropolises Portland and Salem, and the Columbia Plateau in northern Oregon. These temperate rain forests contain bigleaf maples, Douglas fir, and western hemlock, some of the oldest and tallest trees in the Pacific Northwest, alongside some of the most beautiful waterfalls in the U.S.

Map of Oregon

Crater Lake

Crater Lake reaches depths of 1,943 feet, making it the deepest lake in the United States. It is also one of the most beautiful, with a vivid blue color that comes from the depth and purity of the water.

The lake is the main attraction of Oregon's Crater Lake National Park and partly fills a caldera left by the collapse of the volcano, Mount Mazama, 7,700 years ago. The lake is considered to be one of the cleanest lakes in the United States; no rivers feed into it and so the lake's water is only replenished by rain and snowfall. There is a variety of outdoor activities offered by the lake and the surrounding park, including swimming, boat tours, biking, hiking, and fishing.

Best time to visit: The park is open year-round, but the north entrance closes during the winter and does not open again until the spring. The south and west entrances are open year-round.

Pass/Permit/Fees: Refer to State Parks' website.

Closest city or town: Prospect

How to get there: From Klamath Falls, take Hwy. 97 to Hwy. 62 to the park's south entrance.

GPS Coordinates: 42.9446° N, 122.1090° W

Did You Know? One notable aspect of Crater Lake is the famous "Old Man of the Lake," a large tree that has been floating vertically in the lake for over a century.

Journal:

Date(s) Visited:

Weather conditions:

Who you were with:

Nature observations:

Special memories:

Painted Hills

At first glance, Oregon's Painted Hills look, well, painted, but the stripes of red, tan, orange, and black actually chronicle the shifting climate of prehistoric times. This colorful geological site is part of the John Day Fossil Beds National Monument and was once an ancient floodplain. The multicolored effect originated thirty-five million years ago as the climate of the area changed over time.

The Painted Hills section of the monument offers five hiking trails, but be sure to check out the other two sections of the Fossil Beds: the Clarno and Sheep Rock units. Wrap the visit up with a quick trip to the Thomas Condon Paleontology and Visitor Center, where you can view over 500 fossil specimens.

Best time to visit: The Painted Hills section of the Fossil Beds is open year-round from sunrise to sunset and best photographed in the late afternoon.

Pass/Permit/Fees: Entry is free.

Closest city or town: Mitchell

How to get there: From Bend: Head north on Hwy. 97. Head east on Hwy. 26 towards Mitchell. Drive through the Ochoco National Forest and look for brown signs mentioning the Painted Hills.

GPS Coordinates: 44.6615° N, 120.2731° W

Did You Know? The Painted Hills unit of the Fossil Beds is especially important to vertebrate paleontologists due to an abundance of fossils of early horses, rhinoceroses, and even camels.

Journal:

Date(s) Visited:

Weather conditions:

Who you were with:

Nature observations:

Special memories:

Smith Rock

Not many places can claim to be the birthplace of a sport, but the American sport of climbing was born at Smith Rock, a natural playground for thrill-seekers of all types! Smith Rock itself is a 3,200-foot-high ridge with a sheer cliff face overlooking the Crooked River. The volcanic rock is made out of layers of tuff, a type of rock made from volcanic ash, from approximately thirty million years ago, as well as more recent layers of basalt (another igneous rock) from approximately half a million years ago.

Even if you're not much of a climber, Smith Rock offers opportunities for hiking and mountain biking. Keep your eyes peeled and you might see a golden eagle, prairie falcon, or river otter in their natural habitat as well!

Best time to visit: The park is open year-round from dawn to dusk, but some climbing areas are closed or have limited access from about January 15 to August 1 to protect nesting raptors.

Pass/Permit/Fees: A $5 day use permit is required per vehicle. If you are camping at the park, that fee is covered by your camping receipt.

Closest city or town: Terrebonne

How to get there: From Bend, take US-97 North toward Redmond for about 22 miles. Follow signs for the State Park from there.

GPS Coordinates: 44.3682° N, 121.1406° W

Did You Know? The State Park has over 1,800 rock climbing routes as of 2010.

Journal:

Date(s) Visited:

Weather conditions:

Who you were with:

Nature observations:

Special memories:

No Name Lake

This "lake without a name" is one of Oregon's best kept secrets, located amidst the snowy peaks of the Cascade Mountain Range. During spring and summer, the pure turquoise waters of the lake sparkle in the sunshine, and the view of Broken Top Mountain, the Three Sisters, and Oregon's valleys and forests isn't too bad either.

One thing that keeps the lake so remote is that it is only accessible by foot. The hike itself is around 15 miles, offers very little cover from the Oregon sun, and the last stretch requires you to scramble up a very steep creek bed. It is important to bring plenty of fluids and make sure you are prepared.

Best time to visit: Due to its elevation, this area is generally only open from April to October and is blanketed in snow the rest of the year. If you are hoping to catch the lake surrounded by Oregon's wildflowers, you'll want to visit during the summer, though you might also run into some mosquitos.

Pass/Permit/Fees: Visit recreation.gov for more information.

Closest city or town: Bend

How to get there: From Bend: Head west on the Cascade Lakes Hwy. for 24 miles. Take a right onto Rd. 4600-380 to the Todd Lake trailhead.

GPS Coordinates: 44.0809° N, 121.6871° W

Did You Know? While camping used to be permitted next to the lake, a new rule went into effect in 2019 that restricts camping in the lake's basin or within a quarter mile of it.

Journal:

Date(s) Visited:

Weather conditions:

Who you were with:

Nature observations:

Special memories:

Neskowin Ghost Forest

The Neskowin Ghost Forest is one of Oregon's wonders that manages to be both new and immensely old. The stumps that make up the forest were once Sitka spruce trees, many of which are over two thousand years old and were once 150-200 feet high. However, the stumps remained buried under the sand of Oregon's Tillamook Coast until 1997-1998, when powerful winter storms eroded enough of the coastline to reveal what had been hidden.

The geologists who studied the Ghost Forest speculate that some natural disaster — likely the earthquake that hit the Cascadia subduction zone in 1700 — led to the trees being swiftly buried. Today, they are a dramatic and mysterious sight to behold, with one hundred stumps crusted in marine life spread out on the beach.

Best time to visit: The forest is accessible year-round and best viewed at low tide, with January-March seeing the lowest tides.

Pass/Permit/Fees: Entry is free.

Closest city or town: Neskowin

How to get there: From Lincoln City: Take Oregon Coast Hwy./US-101 north for 13 miles. Exit at Summit Rd. and follow the signs. The beach is a five minute walk from the public parking lot.

GPS Coordinates: 45.1034° N, 123.9809° W

Did You Know? The Ghost Forest is near Proposal Rock, an island off of Tillamook Coast named for a local legend where sea captain Charles Gage asked his sweetheart Della Page to marry him.

Journal:

Date(s) Visited:

Weather conditions:

Who you were with:

Nature observations:

Special memories:

Metolius Balancing Rocks

The location of the Balancing Rocks in Cove Palisades State Park was once a well-kept park ranger secret. The Park Service feared that the precariously perched rocks would attract vandals, and so the location was not publicized on any maps. In 2002, that changed when a wildfire decimated the overgrown juniper-pine forest that concealed the rocks. With the rocks no longer hidden, park rangers changed their tune and are now glad to direct visitors to the rocks.

The peculiar Balancing Rocks offer a fascinating look into Oregon's volcanic history. The standing spires were created in one volcanic eruption, while the rocks that balance were created in subsequent eruptions. When erosion began, the rocks on top guarded their spires down below, protecting and preserving them.

Best time to visit: The rocks are visible year-round.

Pass/Permit/Fees: Visit https://stateparks.oregon.gov.

Closest city or town: Culver

How to get there: From Bend: Head north on US-97 for 31 miles to Cove Palisades Park. Drive west through Cove Palisades toward Perry South Campground in the Deschutes National Forest for 13 miles. Look for the balancing rocks parking area and trailhead.

GPS Coordinates: N 44° 34.672 W 121° 25.315

Did You Know? The Balancing Rocks Trailhead was built in 2005, three years after the wildfire that exposed the rocks' location and is only about a quarter of a mile long, ending in a scenic overlook where you can feast your eyes on all three spires.

Journal:

Date(s) Visited:

Weather conditions:

Who you were with:

Nature observations:

Special memories:

Lost Lake

When it comes to Lost Lake, located ten miles northwest of the towering Mt. Hood, Mother Nature really put in the extra work. The lake sparkles. The surrounding flora and fauna are colorful and abundant. The list of potential activities is endless.

If you're craving some water fun, the Lost Lake Resort and Campground offers canoeing, kayaking, fishing boats, and paddleboat rentals. If you're more of a landlubber, there are hiking trails ranging from 0.25 miles to 100 miles surrounding the lake, with plenty of opportunities for bird watching, berry picking, and waterfall finding.

Best time to visit: Lost Lake is within the Mt. Hood National Forest; the resort and campground are closed for the winter. Aim for May-June or September if you're looking to avoid the crowds!

Pass/Permit/Fees: There is a day use fee of $9 per vehicle.

Closest city or town: Government Camp

How to get there: From Portland: Head east on Hwy. 84 for 58 miles. Exit at #62 and take Country Club Rd. Turn left on Barrett Dr., then turn right on Tucker Rd. Tucker Rd. eventually intersects with Hwy. 81; take that to the Lost Lake Rd. exit. Lost Lake Rd. dead-ends at the resort.

GPS Coordinates: 45° 29' 20.0000" N 121° 49' 18.9998" W

Did You Know? The Hood River Native Americans called Lost Lake *"E-e-kwahl-a-mat-yam-lshkt,"* which means "heart of the mountains."

Journal:

Date(s) Visited:

Weather conditions:

Who you were with:

Nature observations:

Special memories:

Thor's Well

Thor's Well is sometimes called "the drainpipe of the Pacific" and it's easy to see why! At first glance, it looks like a seemingly bottomless sinkhole. The well is actually just a large hole in the rock that's likely only about twenty feet deep. Some researchers theorize that the well started out as a sea cave that was formed by the waves of the Pacific over time. The roof eventually collapsed and created openings at the top and bottom of the cave, which is what causes the wild spray of the water out of the top of the well.

Thor's Well can be viewed from the parking lot, the designated viewing area at the bottom of the path, or by walking out to the well itself! If you venture out to the rocks, always remain on the land side and use extreme caution. This area of the Oregon Coast can be unpredictable and dangerous; never turn your back on the waves and be careful with your footing.

Best time to visit: Try aiming to arrive one hour before high tide so that you can see the difference that the tide makes. You can check tide times by visiting tides.willyweather.com.

Pass/Permit/Fees: Entry is free.

Closest city or town: Yachats

How to get there: From Yachats: Take US-101 south for three miles.

GPS Coordinates: 44.2784° N, 124.1135° W

Did You Know? At the right time of year, the Cape Perpetua Visitor Center is a great place to watch the migrating gray whales.

Journal:

Date(s) Visited:

Weather conditions:

Who you were with:

Nature observations:

Special memories:

Proxy Falls

Oregon might be full of waterfalls, but Proxy Falls, tucked away in Willamette National Forest, really steals the show. It's a brief, easy hike just off of the scenic McKenzie Hwy. 242 that offers you the option of hiking to the top of the falls or hiking down to look up the two-hundred-foot drop. Dogs are welcome on the trail, too!

If hiking down to the Lower Falls, exercise caution! The spray from the water can make the rocks slippery. If you have small children, you may want to opt to hike only to the Upper Falls.

Best time to visit: Hwy. 242 closes during the winter, typically November-June. Bicycle access is still possible during that time. Visit tripcheck.com for road and highway conditions.

Pass/Permit/Fees: There is a day use fee of $5 per vehicle and between Memorial Day and Halloween, you must obtain a self-issue wilderness permit; the reservation fee is $1 per person.

Closest city or town: McKenzie Bridge

How to get there: From Eugene: Head east on Hwy. 126. Once you pass the McKenzie River Ranger Station, take a right at the sign for Scenic Hwy. 242. Park alongside the road at the hiker symbol sign between mileposts 64 and 65.

GPS Coordinates: 44.1618° N, 121.9278° W

Did You Know? With a main drop of 226 feet, Proxy Falls is one of the highest plunge waterfalls in the state of Oregon.

Date(s) visited:

28

Journal:

Date(s) Visited:

Weather conditions:

Who you were with:

Nature observations:

Special memories:

Old Fort Road Gravity Hill

While many of Oregon's wonders require a decent time commitment, the gravity hill on Old Fort Road will only take a few minutes of your time, making it a great spot to hit when heading somewhere else. The puzzle of gravity hills — where gravity seems to work in reverse — may be explained by magnetic fields or optical illusions, but watching water run uphill is unsettling, nonetheless.

Local legends about the hill vary wildly, with some insisting that the hill is haunted by spirits from the nearby World War II military medical base and others claiming that the road was paved over an old Native American burial ground.

Best time to visit: The gravity hill's effect can best be seen at nighttime.

Pass/Permit/Fees: None required

Closest city or town: Klamath Falls

How to get there: From Klamath Falls: Head north on OR-39 for about 0.3 miles. Turn right onto OR-97 and then turn right onto Main St. From there turn left onto North Laguna St. and then turn right onto Old Fort Rd. and drive just over a mile. The phenomenon occurs about 50 yards up the hill to the east from an old gravel quarry.

GPS Coordinates: 42.2517 ° N, -121.7426 ° W

Did You Know? The opposite phenomenon of a gravity hill — an uphill path that appears as if it is flat — is called a "false flat."

Journal:

Date(s) Visited:

Weather conditions:

Who you were with:

Nature observations:

Special memories:

Lava River Cave

Oregon is known for its coastlines, dense forests, and snow-capped mountains, but the Oregon underground can be just as fun to explore. Lava River Cave is part of the Newberry National Volcanic Monument and its northwest passage is the longest continuous lava tube in Oregon at 5,211 feet. The cave was formed in a volcanic eruption nearly 80,000 years ago and created when newer layers of lava crusted over the top of the lava river, sealing it inside.

Exploring the cave takes 1.5 hours and the average temperature inside the cave is 42ºF. Two light sources are recommended for the safest exploration of the cave, and the path alternates between stairways, flat boardwalk, and uneven surfaces.

Best time to visit: The Lava River Cave is open from May to September and closed in the winter.

Pass/Permit/Fees: There is a $5 day pass fee to visit the cave. Light sources can be rented for $5 until 4 p.m.

Closest city or town: Bend

How to get there: From Bend: Head south on Hwy. 97. Take Exit 151 at Cottonwood Rd. Turn left after exiting and proceed through the underpass, following signs for Lava River Cave. The entrance is one mile down the road on your left.

GPS Coordinates: 43.8955° N, 121.3697° W

Did You Know? Exploring the last 310 feet of the cave requires crawling on your hands and knees and takes at least 30 minutes.

Journal:

Date(s) Visited:

Weather conditions:

Who you were with:

Nature observations:

Special memories:

Haystack Rock

Towering over visitors at a whopping 235 feet, Haystack Rock is a fifteen-million-year-old sea stack made of volcanic basalt and one of Oregon's more iconic landmarks. The rock was formed by lava flows from the Blue Mountains and was once attached to the coastline, but now stands separate due to the millions of years of erosion.

Many different kinds of marine life can be viewed while visiting the rock, especially during summer at low tide when tidepools along the beach teem with interesting creatures. The area is popular for picnickers, kite-flyers, and bird-watching enthusiasts. However, climbing the rock and touching the wildlife near it is prohibited.

Best time to visit: Haystack Rock can be seen at all times of the year, but if you're walking out to it, you should wait for low tide!

Pass/Permit/Fees: There is no charge to visit Haystack Rock.

Closest city or town: Cannon Beach

How to get there: From Portland: Head west on US-26 for 73 miles. Head South on US-101 for 4 miles. Take a right onto Sunset Blvd. and a left onto South Hemlock St. Haystack Rock is visible from almost anywhere in Cannon Beach.

GPS Coordinates: 45.8841° N, 123.9686° W

Did You Know? Haystack Rock can famously be seen in the background of the opening scene from *The Goonies* where the Fratellis flee the police. It appears later in the film as well, when Mikey points out rocks in the distance.

Journal:

Date(s) Visited:

Weather conditions:

Who you were with:

Nature observations:

Special memories:

Multnomah Falls

Multnomah Falls has something all the other waterfalls in the state of Oregon don't: the title. At a dizzying 620 feet, it is the tallest waterfall in Oregon. According to a legend from the local Multnomah tribe, the waterfall was formed after the self-sacrifice of a young woman who pleaded with the Great Spirit to save her village from plague; she jumped from the cliff and the water began to flow from above.

From the Multnomah Falls Visitor Center, follow the steep trail across Benson Bridge, which crosses about one hundred and five feet over the lower cascade. If you're feeling adventurous, continue to follow the trail up to a small viewing area at the very top of the falls, which offers a bird's-eye view of the Columbia River Gorge.

Best time to visit: To avoid crowds, aim for the fall or winter. In the fall, the sun filters through the golden maples which frame the cascade; in the winter, icy temperatures can freeze the flow entirely, making for an unforgettable winter wonderland.

Pass/Permit/Fees: Entry is free.

Closest city or town: Cascade Locks

How to get there: From Portland: Head east on Interstate 84 for 28 miles. Get off at Exit 31, Multnomah Falls. Park and walk to the Lodge and Visitor Center.

GPS Coordinates: 45.5762° N, 122.1158° W

Did You Know? Multnomah Falls is the most-visited natural site in the Pacific Northwest, attracting over two million visits every year.

Journal:

Date(s) Visited:

Weather conditions:

Who you were with:

Nature observations:

Special memories:

Neahkahnie Mountain

Climb to the summit of Neahkahnie Mountain and you'll understand why it is named "the place of the god" in Tillamook. Standing at 1,661 feet, you are standing at one of the highest points on the Oregon Coast with an incredible view of the sandy shores and the Pacific Ocean. The hike up to the top requires you to scramble up rocks and navigate some tricky twists and turns, but there is a shorter hike that still features some astounding views.

Legend tells of buried treasure on the mountain, carried ashore from a Spanish galleon by sailors, one of whom was allegedly stabbed by his comrades and thrown down into the hole on top of the treasure, the idea being that the dead body would make the spot a burial site which the Native Americans would not disturb. Sadly, no treasure has been found.

Best time to visit: In the springtime, the hike offers views of colorful wildflowers. Aim for a clear day to best see the coastline!

Pass/Permit/Fees: Entry is free.

Closest city or town: Manzanita

How to get there: From Manzanita: Head north for 2.5 miles on US-101. Look for the Oregon Coast Trail sign and the gravel road.

GPS Coordinates: 45.7440° N, 123.9410° W

Did You Know? Oswald West State Park, where Neahkahnie Mountain is located, is named for the fourteenth governor of Oregon. West's legacy includes the preservation of Oregon's beaches for public use.

Journal:

Date(s) Visited:

Weather conditions:

Who you were with:

Nature observations:

Special memories:

Crack in the Ground

The "crack" is actually an ancient volcanic fissure formed thousands of years ago when four volcanoes erupted, creating the Four Craters Lava Field, a shallow depression in the earth. The crack runs along the western edge for over two miles and is seventy feet deep.

Hikers can explore the main fissure and the various crevices, caves, and formations that split off. It is a moderate hike, with some sandy and rocky areas and sharp lava rocks that can be dangerous. There are primitive campsites on Green Mountain near the fissure, as well as a picnic area.

Best time to visit: The trail through the fissure is open year-round, but access might require a four-wheel drive in the winter. In the summer, it can reach temperatures of 95ºF, so make sure to bring plenty of water.

Pass/Permit/Fees: Entry is free.

Closest city or town: Christmas Valley

How to get there: From Christmas Valley: Head east on the Christmas Valley Hwy. for about one mile. Take a left onto Crack in the Ground Road and continue for about seven miles, following signs to Crack in the Ground.

GPS Coordinates: 43.3336° N, 120.6723° W

Did You Know? The temperature in the fissure can be twenty to thirty degrees cooler than on the surface.

Journal:

Date(s) Visited:

Weather conditions:

Who you were with:

Nature observations:

Special memories:

Mount Thielsen Fulgurites

Mount Thielsen, an extinct shield volcano, is known as the "lightning rod of the Cascades," with a pointed top that was worn away over time by glaciers and makes the perfect target for lightning during a storm. In fact, Mount Thielsen gets struck by lightning so frequently that the pinnacle of the mountain is covered in fulgurite. These are sculptures that the lightning creates when it strikes sand or certain kinds of rock; the temperature is so hot that whatever is struck melts and fuses into glass.

It's a tough climb up Mount Thielsen, but it's not impossible! Make sure to properly plan for the climb and bring the necessary gear. If that doesn't sound like your thing, don't fret! The view from below isn't too bad either.

Best time to visit: If you're going to attempt to summit Mount Thielsen, aim for late spring or early fall.

Pass/Permit/Fees: There is a $5 day-use parking fee. A parking permit is required in the winter; a one-day permit is $4.

Closest city or town: Roseburg

How to get there: Head east on OR-138 E/NE Diamond Lake Boulevard. Follow Hwy 138 east to milepost 81.5. The Mt. Thielsen Trailhead parking lot is located on the east side of Hwy 138.

GPS Coordinates: 43.1516° N, 122.0664° W

Did You Know? The material that composes the fulgurites is known as lechatelierite, which can only be formed if the lightning strikes sand that is nearly pure silica.

Journal:

Date(s) Visited:

Weather conditions:

Who you were with:

Nature observations:

Special memories:

Mt. Hood

The official title of Oregon's tallest mountain goes to this potentially active stratovolcano that boasts North America's only year-round lift-served skiing. Don't let the term "potentially active" throw you, though! The odds of an eruption in the next thirty years are estimated at 3-7% and the mountain is informally considered to be dormant.

While experienced climbers might want to make the climb to the top, Mt. Hood offers a variety of outdoor recreation, including skiing, snowboarding, mountain biking, whitewater rafting, and camping.

Best time to visit: Mt. Hood is a popular spot, so avoid summer and spring break if you're looking for some peace and quiet!

Pass/Permit/Fees: For information about the different kinds of permits needed, visit fs.usda.gov.

Closest city or town: Mount Hood Village

How to get there: From Portland: Head north on I-405. Head south on I-5. Head east on I-84 for about seven miles. Take exit 16 and follow signs for US-26 E. Head east on US-26 for about 40 miles. Head north on OR-35 for six miles and take the exit for Ski Resort/Bennet Pass/Soo Park/Mt Hood Meadows. Follow the signs to Mt. Hood National Forest.

GPS Coordinates: 45.3736° N, 121.6960° W

Did You Know? Around 10,000 people attempt to climb Mt. Hood every year.

Journal:

Date(s) Visited:

Weather conditions:

Who you were with:

Nature observations:

Special memories:

Hells Canyon

When European adventurers and homesteaders first stumbled upon the ancestral Nez Perce homeland in the 19th century, they took one look at the rattlesnake-infested, sweltering river gorge and decided they must be in Hell. To this day, Hells Canyon is one of Oregon's more remote locations; no roads cross the canyon and many of its points can only be reached on foot.

The canyon can be viewed from its many trails or from the Snake River itself on one of the many whitewater rafting trips offered by private companies. If you're short on time, there's always the Hells Canyon Scenic Byway, which can be driven in four to five hours.

Best time to visit: Recreation season runs late spring to November.

Pass/Permit/Fees: Many activities in Hells Canyon require permits. Visit fs.usda.gov for more information.

Closest city or town: Halfway

How to get there: From Baker City: Head east on Interstate 84 and enter the Byway by taking exit 304 and following the signs to Oregon Hwy. 86. From there, follow the signs to Hells Canyon.

GPS Coordinates: 45.5158° N, 116.7567° W

Did You Know? Hells Canyon is North America's deepest river gorge; at 7,993 feet, it is even deeper than the Grand Canyon.

Journal:

Date(s) Visited:

Weather conditions:

Who you were with:

Nature observations:

Special memories:

Alvord Desert

The Alvord Desert was once a lake that extended over one hundred miles, but today it is a cold desert surrounded by three different mountain ranges (the Cascades, the Steens, and the Coast Range), that sees only about seven inches of rain a year on average.

The desert is approximately twelve miles long and seven miles wide. Camping is free on the playa but watch out! Driving at very high speeds across the flat is a popular recreational activity, and land speed records are attempted from time to time. Also worth seeing is the desert's geothermal features, including a few different hot springs.

Best time to visit: Winter is very cold, summer is very warm, and spring is very rainy. The ideal time to visit is in the autumn.

Pass/Permit/Fees: Entry is free.

Closest city or town: Fields

How to get there: From Burns: Take US-78/Steens Hwy. east 65 miles to Folly Farm Rd./Fields-Denio Rd. Drive south for 42 miles. There are several dirt access roads to the desert.

GPS Coordinates: 42.5354° N, 118.4560° W

Did You Know? The desert is named for General Benjamin Alvord, a Civil War commander who headed up the U.S. Army's Department of Oregon.

Journal:

Date(s) Visited:

Weather conditions:

Who you were with:

Nature observations:

Special memories:

The Dunes

Oregon's dunes tower up to 500 feet above sea level and stretch for 40 miles along Oregon's Coast, from North Bend to Florence. They were created by wind and water over a long period of time, with sand from the ocean floor being deposited on the shore by the tides and then blown upwards and away by the wind.

There's a lot to do besides view the dunes from the Oregon Dunes Overlook just south of Dune City! There are three main areas approved for off-highway vehicle use, and lots of rivers, lakes, and the Pacific Ocean for those interested in water sports. If you're feeling contemplative, there are a variety of trails to hike as well.

Best time to visit: If you come between March and September, be sure to check which areas are protected for nesting snowy plovers!

Pass/Permit/Fees: There is a $5 day use fee. Some activities may require a permit. Visit fs.usda.gov for more information.

Closest city or town: Florence or Dune City

How to get there: From Reedsport: Head north on Hwy. 101 for 11 miles. The entrance to the Oregon Dunes Day Use is located on the west side of Hwy. 101 near mile marker 201.

GPS Coordinates: 43.7035° N, 124.1060° W

Did You Know? The famous science fiction setting of Arrakis in *Dune* by Frank Herbert was partly inspired by the Oregon dunes.

Journal:

Date(s) Visited:

Weather conditions:

Who you were with:

Nature observations:

Special memories:

Silver Falls

Silver Falls State Park is home to the Trail of Ten Falls, a nationally recognized seven-mile hike that leads you through a dense forest up to — and sometimes behind — ten beautiful waterfalls, ranging from the 27-foot Drake Falls to the 177-foot remote South Falls.

The hike is classified as moderate, so if that's not your thing, check out South Falls from the viewing bridge or visit the Silver Falls Riding Stables for a guided horseback ride. There are also picnic areas, barbecue stands, and off-leash areas near a little creek in the South Falls day-use area.

Best time to visit: This park is one of the easier parks to visit in winter since it doesn't get too snowy, but the falls are still full and the wildflowers are at their best from late March to May.

Pass/Permit/Fees: There is a $5 day-use parking fee.

Closest city or town: Silverton

How to get there: From Silverton: Take OR-214 south for 13 miles and follow signs for Silver Falls State Park.

GPS Coordinates: 44.8652° N, 122.6262° W

Did You Know? Silver Falls State Park is the largest state park in Oregon and was used as a filming location for several blockbuster films, including *The Hunted* and *Twilight*.

Journal:

Date(s) Visited:

Weather conditions:

Who you were with:

Nature observations:

Special memories:

Blue Basin

The Blue Basin is actually found near one of the wonders mentioned earlier in the book! This site is located at the John Day Fossil Beds National Monument which also features Oregon's Painted Hills. The Blue Basin is part of the Sheep Rock unit.

The blue color derives from volcanic ash that turned to claystone and then eroded over millions of years. The Island in Time Trail, which is about one and a half miles roundtrip, takes you through the Basin, while the Blue Basin Overlook Trail offers a longer hike, just over three miles, and stunning views.

Best time to visit: Since the trails offer very little in terms of shade, aim for a cloudy day or get started in the morning. Bring plenty of water if hiking in the summer!

Pass/Permit/Fees: Entry is free.

Closest city or town: Mitchell

How to get there: From Bend: Head North on Hwy. 97. Head east on Hwy. 26 towards Mitchell. Drive through the Ochoco National Forest and look for the brown signs mentioning Sheep Rock.

GPS Coordinates: 44.5912° N, 119.6177° W

Did You Know? While no natural fossil specimens are visible from these trails, the Island in Time Trail winds alongside three replica fossils embedded in stone.

Journal:

Date(s) Visited:

Weather conditions:

Who you were with:

Nature observations:

Special memories:

Fort Rock

About 100,000 years ago, basalt magma from beneath the Earth's surface pushed through what is now known as Fort Rock Lake and created a ring of tuff around half a mile in diameter. Over millennia, waves from the lake wore away at the ring until it was shaped into a jagged formation with straight sides that inspired settler William Sullivan to name the structure "Fort Rock" in 1873.

Fort Rock now looms up to 300 feet above the dry lakebed covered in sage and brush. It is also home to some of the oldest-known human artifacts in North America. Archaeologists have discovered a variety of woven sandals estimated between 9,000 and 13,000 years old.

Best time to visit: There is not much in terms of shade, so aim for a cloudy day or visit in the morning to avoid the heat of the sun.

Pass/Permit/Fees: Entry is free.

Closest city or town: Christmas Valley

How to get there: From Bend: Head south on US-97 for 60 miles. Continue on County Rd. 5-10 for six miles then drive to County Road 5-11A and follow the signs for Fort Rock State Natural Area.

GPS Coordinates: 43.3568° N, 121.0548° W

Did You Know? The community of Fort Rock, Oregon, is one of two homestead-era communities that remain in this area of Oregon, the other being Silver Lake.

Journal:

Date(s) Visited:

Weather conditions:

Who you were with:

Nature observations:

Special memories:

The Octopus Tree

This 105-foot tree has also been called the Candelabra Tree, the Monstrosity Tree, and the Council Tree. It has no central trunk; instead, the tree base splits into six limbs that extend out up to 16 feet before shooting upwards, giving the tree the appearance of an inverted octopus. There are several different theories on how the tree came to be shaped. Some suggest it was done by extreme wind, while local historians believe that it was done by Native Americans who shaped the tree for burial purposes, to hold canoes filled with corpses.

The hike to the tree is less than half a mile through Cape Meares State Park and the Scenic Viewpoint nearby offers a beautiful view of the Pacific Ocean 200 feet above the surf.

Best time to visit: Visit during the spring or winter to catch an incredible view of migrating gray whales from the Scenic Viewpoint.

Pass/Permit/Fees: Entry is free.

Closest city or town: Tillamook

How to get there: From Tillamook: Head west on OR-131 for 10 miles. Turn left onto Bayshore Dr. and in one mile turn right onto Cape Meares Lighthouse Dr.

GPS Coordinates: N 45°29′04.0 W123°58′21.0

Did You Know? Trees that were shaped by Native Americans are known as culturally modified trees, common in the Pacific Northwest.

Journal:

Date(s) Visited:

Weather conditions:

Who you were with:

Nature observations:

Special memories:

Pillars of Rome

Rome wasn't built in a day, and neither were these towering clay cliffs! They are remnants from Oregon's violent volcanic age and were formed by volcanic ash that eroded over time. They stand one hundred feet tall, stretch for five miles, and are so distinct that they were used as landmarks for settlers braving the Oregon Trail.

Bring your camera to snap a few panoramic shots, but be careful when approaching the Pillars, as slabs of rock could break off and fall with any movement.

Best time to visit: The lighting for photographs is best in the late afternoon, leading up to sunset.

Pass/Permit/Fees: Entry is free.

Closest city or town: Jordan Valley

How to get there: From Burns: Head east on OR-78 for 100 miles. Once you have arrived in Rome, take the dirt road across from the Rome store. Follow the road for two miles, then take a right and then a left. Continue to the west and park your car a distance from the Pillars.

GPS Coordinates: 42.8579° N, 117.6841° W

Did You Know? The rock formations were named by homesteader William F. Stine, who remarked on their resemblance to the ruins of old Roman temples and buildings.

Journal:

Date(s) Visited:

Weather conditions:

Who you were with:

Nature observations:

Special memories:

Sea Lion Cave

Well, technically it's a series of interconnected caves and caverns, but these caves, located around the midpoint of the Oregon Coast, are the year-round home of the Steller sea lion (though the California sea lion has been known to make an appearance).

An elevator will take you down to the cave where you can see the sea lions themselves. This area of the coast is also home to lots of other coastal animals, like sea birds, and you can view migrating gray whales and orcas from the whale watching deck.

Best time to visit: The sea lions come and go as they please, so the wildlife preserve recommends calling ahead for the status of the sea lions. In the late fall, they are often absent for long periods of time.

Pass/Permit/Fees: Adult tickets are $14. Senior tickets are $13. Children (ages 5-12) tickets are $8. Children under 4 enter for free. There is no parking fee.

Closest city or town: Florence

How to get there: From Florence: Head north on US-101 for 10 miles and follow the signs for Sea Lion Caves.

GPS Coordinates: 44.1218° N, 124.1267° W

Did You Know? Captain William Cox was the first to discover the caves by entering the grotto on a small boat. He reportedly made several visits to the caves, once marooning himself for several days during a storm.

Journal:

Date(s) Visited:

Weather conditions:

Who you were with:

Nature observations:

Special memories:

Clear Lake

Clear Lake was named for its incredible purity and only a glimpse is needed to see why. Formed in a volcanic eruption 3,000 years ago, the lake is so cold that a grove of preserved upright trees that were killed in the eruption is still standing. Take a canoe or kayak out to the middle of the lake, and you can see straight down to the enchanting forest. Experienced divers can even dive down and check the trees out up close.

There are two trails near Clear Lake; the Clear Lake Loop Trail is a flat, pet- and family-friendly lap around the lake's perimeter. The McKenzie River trail is much more difficult, a 26-mile destination trail that attracts hikers and mountain bikers alike. Rent a canoe or kayak from the local Clear Lake Resort to explore the 142-acre lake or visit the general store for a picnic on the lake's shore!

Best time to visit: The water of Clear Lake hovers just above freezing year-round due to its high altitude at 3,000 feet above sea level.

Pass/Permit/Fees: Some trails or day-use sites may require a recreation pass. Visit fs.usda.gov for more details.

Closest city or town: McKenzie Bridge

How to get there: From McKenzie Bridge: Head east on Hwy. 126 for 18 miles to Clear Lake.

GPS Coordinates: 44.3687° N, 121.9944° W

Did You Know? Clear Lake is the headwaters of the McKenzie River, which provides all of the drinking water for Eugene, Oregon.

Journal:

Date(s) Visited:

Weather conditions:

Who you were with:

Nature observations:

Special memories:

Tamolitch Blue Pool

Nearly 1600 years ago, the Belknap Crater released a lava flow that buried a three-mile stretch of the McKenzie River deep underground. The Blue Pool was created by water flowing up through those underground lava tubes which gives the water its unique turquoise hue.

A two-mile hike on a well-maintained trail leads you to look out over the Blue Pool. The water is very cold, hovering around 40ºF year-round, so swimming is not recommended. The pool is deceptively deep at 30 feet, and several people have died jumping into or falling into the pool. Instead, bring your lunch and have a picnic at the top of the rocks while enjoying the incredible view.

Best time to visit: This hike experiences lots of foot traffic, especially in the spring and summer. Visit in spring to get the best chance of water runoff being high enough to waterfall into the Blue Pool.

Pass/Permit/Fees: Entry is free.

Closest city or town: McKenzie Bridge

How to get there: From McKenzie Bridge: Head east on OR-126 for 13 miles to Trail Bridge Reservoir. Turn left on FS Rd. 730. Cross the river and turn right on FS Rd. 2672-655; the parking area is half a mile down.

GPS Coordinates: 44.3123° N, 122.0272° W

Did You Know? Tamolitch is a Chinook word that means "bucket."

Journal:

Date(s) Visited:

Weather conditions:

Who you were with:

Nature observations:

Special memories:

Waldo Lake

Waldo Lake is the second deepest lake in Oregon with a maximum depth of 420 feet, losing only to Crater Lake, which has a maximum depth of 1,949. Just like Crater Lake, the water at Waldo is so clear that you can see depths of up to 120 feet on a clear day. Conservationists have taken many steps to preserve the water purity of Waldo Lake, including banning motorized boats powered by gasoline and limiting the top speed of boats with electric motors.

Waldo Lake is a popular site for various water recreational activities, including swimming, canoeing, kayaking, and sailing.

Best time to visit: Late summer and early fall often mean that the campgrounds nearby are booked full, so aim to visit in spring instead!

Pass/Permit/Fees: Some trails and day-use activities may require a recreation pass. Visit fs.usda.gov for more details.

Closest city or town: Crescent Lake Junction

How to get there: From Crescent Lake Junction: Head north on OR-58 W for 12 miles. Turn right onto NF-5897 and follow for eight miles.

GPS Coordinates: 43.7270° N, 122.0445° W

Did You Know? The lake is named after John B. Waldo, an Oregon politician and judge who advocated for conservation of the land.

Journal:

Date(s) Visited:

Weather conditions:

Who you were with:

Nature observations:

Special memories:

Table Rock

Just outside of Medford stand two volcanic plateaus that are nearly seven million years old, called Oregon's "Islands in the Sky." Upper Table Rock and Lower Table Rock were created by lava flow and then shaped by erosion over time. The tops of the two plateaus feature vernal pools that fill with rainwater due to the impermeable nature of the andesite that forms the structures. These pools are home to the fairy shrimp, which is a threatened species.

There are two trails to hike up to Table Rock, but the path to Upper Table Rock is shorter and slightly easier, though the path to Lower Table Rock is slightly shadier.

Best time to visit: Visit during April or May to see the over two hundred different species of wildflowers in bloom!

Pass/Permit/Fees: Entry is free.

Closest city or town: Medford

How to get there: From Medford: Take Biddle Rd. 3.5 miles then turn right onto Table Rock Rd. and follow for six miles.

GPS Coordinates: 42.4513° N, 122.9126° W

Did You Know? Upper Table Rock and Lower Table Rock were once inhabited by the Takelma Native Americans. During a gold rush, the area was quickly developed and the Takelma were forced onto reservations.

Journal:

Date(s) Visited:

Weather conditions:

Who you were with:

Nature observations:

Special memories:

Mount McLoughlin

Mount McLoughlin is one of the volcanic peaks of the Cascade Range. It's a dormant stratovolcano and major landmark for the Rogue River Valley in Oregon, with an elevation of 9,493 feet.

There is a five-mile hiking trail to the summit of Mount McLoughlin, which typically requires six hours to hike. The trail ascends through rocky terrain and can be difficult to follow but is considered non-technical with a rewarding view at the end.

Best time to visit: The trail is open from summer to fall, and snow can appear on the mountain at any time of year.

Pass/Permit/Fees: Entry is free.

Closest city or town: Klamath Falls

How to get there: From Klamath Falls: head west on Hwy. 140 for 35 miles. Turn right on Forest Rd. 3661 (Four Mile Lake Rd.) and follow for 2.4 miles to Forest Rd. 3650, turning left. The parking is 0.25 mile down.

GPS Coordinates: 42.4449° N, 122.3153° W

Did You Know? The three Native American tribes that lived at the foot of Mt. McLoughlin — the Klamath, the Shasta, and the Takelma — each had different names for the mountain, which were often important in their stories and traditions.

Journal:

Date(s) Visited:

Weather conditions:

Who you were with:

Nature observations:

Special memories:

Umpqua National Forest

The Umpqua National Forest has three different Wilderness areas: Boulder Creek Wilderness, Mount Thielsen Wilderness, and Rogue Umpqua Divide Wilderness.

The Umpqua National Forest offers camping, over 300 miles of trail maintained for year-round use, and fishing at Diamond Lake. The Forest has several waterfalls including the 272-foot Watson Falls. Or enjoy the Forest without the fuss and drive down the Rogue-Umpqua National Scenic Byway for a great view!

Best time to visit: Visit during the fall to see the autumn foliage.

Pass/Permit/Fees: Some activities may require a recreation pass. Visit fs.usda.gov for more details.

Closest city or town: Roseburg

How to get there: From Roseburg: Head east on OR-138 for 16 miles. Turn right onto Little River Rd. and follow for six miles. Turn left onto BLM Rd. 32/2/Thunder Mountain Rd. and follow for 12 miles.

GPS Coordinates: 43.2189° N, 122.6193° W

Did You Know? The word Umpqua can translate to either "thundering waters" or "across the waters," but another translation is "satisfied," referring to a full stomach.

Journal:

Date(s) Visited:

Weather conditions:

Who you were with:

Nature observations:

Special memories:

Cape Meares

Cape Meares features some of Oregon's most incredible views. In fact, most of the cape is part of the Cape Meares State Scenic Viewpoint, which offers three miles of hiking trails up to the top of the bluff. Gaze at the Oregon Coast before heading to Cape Meares Lighthouse and taking a free tour.

In addition to the baffling Octopus Tree, Cape Meares is home to the Big Spruce, Oregon's largest Sitka tree at 144 feet.

Best time to visit: Visit from April to July for the best chance at spotting migrating gray whales and nesting seabirds in the cliffs and offshore rocks.

Pass/Permit/Fees: Entry is free.

Closest city or town: Tillamook

How to get there: From Tillamook: Head west on OR-131 for 10 miles. Turn left onto Bayshore Dr. and in one mile, turn right onto Cape Meares Lighthouse Dr.

GPS Coordinates: 45.4898° N, 123.9587° W

Did You Know? Cape Meares Lighthouse is the shortest lighthouse on the Oregon Coast at just a mere 38 feet.

Journal:

Date(s) Visited:

Weather conditions:

Who you were with:

Nature observations:

Special memories:

Devil's Churn

Devil's Churn is an inlet that was carved over thousands of years as waves lashed against the basalt shoreline. This formed an underwater sea cave whose roof eventually collapsed. Now, when the tide comes in, Devil's Churn hurls the water several hundred feet in the air!

Visitors are permitted to walk down to the volcanic rock surrounding the churn and can even cross over to the far side, but it's important to be extremely cautious, both with the waves of the Pacific Ocean and with your footing, as the water makes the jagged volcanic rock slippery.

Best time to visit: It is open year-round but, in the winter, the waves of the Pacific Ocean can be especially strong and deadly. Aim for high tide to best see this natural wonder.

Pass/Permit/Fees: There is a $5 day-use parking fee.

Closest city or town: Yachats

How to get there: From Yachats: Take US-101 south for three miles. From Cape Perpetua Scenic Overlook take the Restless Waters Trail.

GPS Coordinates: 44.2846° N, 124.1157° W

Did You Know? Devil's Churn is really more of a Devil's Funnel, but it's easy to see why that name wouldn't have stuck as well.

Journal:

Date(s) Visited:

Weather conditions:

Who you were with:

Nature observations:

Special memories:

Arnold Ice Cave

Just another testament to Oregon's volcanic history is Arnold Ice Cave. The Cave is actually part of a system of caves created in a lava flow. The lava tubes are around 80,000 years old, but Arnold Ice Cave was not discovered by Americans until 1889. Unfortunately, due to vandalism and defacement by climbers, there are large sections of the cave system that conservationists are still attempting to restore to their original state.

Take the Hidden Forest and Arnold Ice Cave Trail down to the cave's entrance and check it out for yourself! This hike falls short of one mile and is good for all skill levels. It offers breathtaking views of Oregon's wildflowers during the spring. Temperatures in the cave hover just above freezing, so dress warmly.

Best time to visit: The cave is closed from November to April to protect the hibernation of the bats that call the cave home.

Pass/Permit/Fees: Entry is free.

Closest city or town: Bend

How to get there: From Bend: Take US-97 south for nearly five miles, exiting onto Knott Rd. and turning left to follow for 1.5 miles. Turn right onto Arnold Ice Cave/China Hat Rd. and follow for 10 miles. Turn right onto Swamp Wells Rd. and drive 0.5 mile to the end of the road. The Ice Cave is to the left of the main trailhead.

GPS Coordinates: N 43° 57' 4.1184", W 121° 15' 4.5648"

Did You Know? The Cave was once used to excavate ice for the nearby town of Bend before electricity was available.

Journal:

Date(s) Visited:

Weather conditions:

Who you were with:

Nature observations:

Special memories:

Natural Bridges Cove

This hidden gem tucked away from the rest of the world is something straight out of a fairy tale! Giant sea arches rise out of the swirling, turquoise water as it enters and exits the cove.

The trail down to the scenic viewing platform features some quick elevation gain at the end, but the trail is well-marked and easy to follow. Once you reach the viewpoint, you're treated with an incredible view. It is possible to reach the natural bridges yourself but it is very dangerous to do so and very easy to slip and fall.

Best time to visit: Visit at sunrise or sunset for the best photography lighting. Visit in spring for a hike through Oregon's wildflowers.

Pass/Permit/Fees: Entry is free.

Closest city or town: Brookings

How to get there: From Brookings: Head north on US-101 for 11 miles and follow signs for the Natural Bridges Cove: North Island Viewpoint parking lot and Trail.

GPS Coordinates: N 42° 11' 24.108", W 124° 21' 57.4194"

Did You Know? Natural Bridges Cove is part of the twenty-mile Samuel H. Boardman State Scenic Corridor which runs alongside Oregon's southern coast.

Journal:

Date(s) Visited:

Weather conditions:

Who you were with:

Nature observations:

Special memories:

Elowah Falls

This 213-foot drop makes one of the most beautiful waterfalls in the Columbia River Gorge. The fall is formed as McCord Creek is forced into a narrow channel of water that shoots out over the walls of basalt that form the sides of the amphitheater.

The trail is fairly easy and appropriate for most skill levels, with a small amount of climbing and then a summit in the middle of the hike. Consider combining the trail with the Upper McCord Creek Falls trail for a longer hike or visit the Cascade Fish Hatchery and take a self-guided tour.

Best time to visit: Visit in early spring for the most photogenic waterfall when heavy seasonal rains cause the waterfalls to rage. There is limited parking that can fill up quickly on weekends.

Pass/Permit/Fees: Entry is free.

Closest city or town: Portland

How to get there: From Portland: Head north on I-405 for just over two miles. Take I-5 south and then take exit 301 for I-84/US-30 and head east for five miles before taking I-84 east for another 32 miles, taking Exit #35/Ainsworth. Turn left at the stop sign, then immediately turn right onto Frontage Rd. Head east on Frontage Rd. for two miles and turn right into the trailhead parking lot.

GPS Coordinates: 45.6119° N, 121.9946° W

Did You Know? Elowah Falls was originally named McCord Falls, but pushback from a mountaineering organization called the Mazamas, led to the name being changed to Elowah.

Journal:

Date(s) Visited:

Weather conditions:

Who you were with:

Nature observations:

Special memories:

Salt Creek Falls

Visit one of Oregon's most powerful waterfalls, tucked away in the Cascade Mountains. There is a viewing platform fifty yards away from the parking lot that is wheelchair accessible. If you're wanting a different vantage point, follow Salt Creeks Fall Trail, a loop gravel trail, or follow a short but steep path down to the waterfall's base. The best view is said to be from halfway down this path! Salt Creek Falls is Oregon's second-highest single-drop waterfall, with a cascade of 286 feet, and its pool reaches depths of sixty-six feet.

The Observation Site also includes a picnic area, so this is a great spot for a light hike and some lunch. If you're craving more of a challenge, try connecting with Diamond Creek Falls Loop Trail for another waterfall view and an extra three miles of hiking.

Best time to visit: The Observation Site is typically closed in winter and the waterfall is the most photogenic in late spring and early summer. Avoid the weekends to avoid the crowds!

Pass/Permit/Fees: There is a $5 day-use parking fee.

Closest city or town: Oakridge

How to get there: From Oakridge: Head east on OR-58 for 22 miles. Turn right onto NF-5893 and follow the signs for Salt Creek Falls. The parking lot is well-signed from the main road.

GPS Coordinates: 43.6120° N, 122.1284° W

Did You Know? Salt Creek Falls is named for its parent stream, whose downstream springs are often used as mineral licks by wildlife.

Journal:

Date(s) Visited:

Weather conditions:

Who you were with:

Nature observations:

Special memories:

Opal Creek

Opal Creek — named by a U.S. Forest Service Ranger who compared it to his wife's beauty — is a pristine stream surrounded by a gigantic forest of trees that range from 450-1,000 years old. It is one of the more remote wildernesses in Oregon.

There are eight trails in the Wilderness, ranging from 2-to-17 miles. For a moderate hike, try the Henline Falls trail with a 1.8-mile out-and-back climb. More experienced hikers may want to tackle the Little North Santiam Trail or the Gate to Jawbone Flats (a Depression-era mining camp) and Opal Pool.

Best time to visit: The trailhead is open all year, but this is a good hike for the summer since the density of the trees keeps the forest cool year-round.

Pass/Permit/Fees: There is a $5 day-use parking fee. Check to see if any permits are applicable to you at fs.usda.gov.

Closest city or town: Detroit

How to get there: From Detroit: Head north on OR-22 W. Turn right on French Creek Rd. and follow for four miles. Turn right onto NF-2207 and follow for 16 miles. Take a right onto NF-2207/NF-2209 and follow for four miles to the locked gate.

GPS Coordinates: 44.859856, -122.264394.

Did You Know? The Opal Creek Wilderness was threatened by the logging industry until 1998, when a wilderness bill twenty years in the making officially protected it as a scenic recreation area.

Journal:

Date(s) Visited:

Weather conditions:

Who you were with:

Nature observations:

Special memories:

Hart's Cove

This beautiful inlet fed by a narrow waterfall (Chitwood Creek Falls) can be reached after a moderate hike through an old Sitka Spruce forest, where some of the trees have been around for 250 years. The area is day-use only, with no overnight parking or camping.

The hike crosses two creeks and ends at a prairie meadow where Oregon's wildflowers can be seen for most of the season. Bring something to eat and settle in for a picnic lunch overlooking the beautiful cove while you listen to the seabirds and sea lions.

Best time to visit: The area is open from July 16 to December 31 and closed the remainder of the year. For the most impressive waterfall view, aim for early summer or late fall.

Pass/Permit/Fees: There is no fee for entry.

Closest city or town: Hebo

How to get there: From Lincoln City: Head north 4.5 miles to the junction of Hwy. 101 and Hwy. 18, then head north three miles to Forest Service Rd. 1861, west of Hwy. 101. The trailhead is located at the end of the road, about four miles.

GPS Coordinates: 45.0748° N, 124.0012° W

Did You Know? Harbor Seals can often be seen in Hart's Cove. Those who feel up to a steep incline can hike past the meadow overlook down to the water.

Journal:

Date(s) Visited:

Weather conditions:

Who you were with:

Nature observations:

Special memories:

Terwilliger Hot Springs

These pristine geothermal pools are natural hot springs, accessed by a quarter-mile trail from the parking lot through the forest, where you are shielded by a canopy of treetops and offered a view of a beautiful lagoon and Rider Creek Falls.

The six pools are clothing optional and range in temperature from 85 to 112ºF. The area is day-use only and alcohol is not permitted.

Best time to visit: The road to the parking lot is not maintained for snow and ice, so it's best to hit this one before it starts to snow in late autumn.

Pass/Permit/Fees: There is a $7 fee for access to the pools, lagoon, trail, and parking lot.

Closest city or town: Blue River

How to get there: From Blue River: Head east on Hwy. 126 for four miles to Aufderheide Scenic Byway. Take Aufderheide Dr. south, taking a right at the Y to the top of Cougar Reservoir. Head south on Aufderheide Dr. for five miles to the parking lot.

GPS Coordinates: 44.0830° N, 122.2384° W

Did You Know? The Terwilliger Hot Springs is also known as the Cougar Hot Springs since the springs drain into Rider Creek, which in turn drains into Cougar Reservoir.

Journal:

Date(s) Visited:

Weather conditions:

Who you were with:

Nature observations:

Special memories:

Owyhee River

The Owyhee River is a tributary of the Snake River, with its headwaters in Nevada but spanning much of Southeastern Oregon. This rugged, remote wilderness attracts rafting and kayaking enthusiasts alongside fishers, hunters, and nature enthusiasts, as the Owyhee Canyonlands are home to over 200 species of wildlife.

There's no doubt about it: the best way to see the Owyhee is to take a guided tour down the river. The most popular trip is 3-5 days and launches out of Rome, Oregon. The temperature of the air and the water is often cold and variable, so take that into consideration when making plans for your trip.

Best time to visit: If taking a trip or tour down the Owyhee, aim for April or May, as the river is not traversable much of the year. Expect weekends to be busy!

Pass/Permit/Fees: Boater registration is mandatory for all boaters prior to launch. Private parties are not required to obtain permits.

Closest city or town: Rome

How to get there: From Jordan Valley: Take US Hwy. 95 southwest for 32 miles and turn south at the Owyhee River and BLM-Rome Boat Launch sign.

GPS Coordinates: 43.8126°N, -117.0254°W

Did You Know? Sacajawea's son Jean Baptiste Charbonneau died after crossing the Owyhee River and his grave is marked off Hwy. 95 in southeast Oregon near Danner.

Journal:

Date(s) Visited:

Weather conditions:

Who you were with:

Nature observations:

Special memories:

Leslie Gulch

One of Oregon's most beautiful canyons, the Gulch, is one of the popular ending spots for a trip down the Owyhee River. It also features some of Oregon's most beautiful rock formations and over eighty established climbing routes. You can hike one of the trails into Juniper Gulch or Timber Gulch or simply admire a few of the rare plants that call this area home.

Camping at the local Slocum Creek Campground is free and first-come, first-served. The area is highly remote, so keep an eye out for ticks, rattlesnakes, and the invasive weed, goat head, whose sharp and rock-hard points can puncture air mattresses and injure your canine friends.

Best time to visit: Flash floods can make the road into the Gulch impassable and, with no cell service or WiFi to call for help, Leslie Gulch is best visited in the dry season, typically summer.

Pass/Permit/Fees: Entry is free.

Closest city or town: Adrian

How to get there: From Jordan Valley: Head north on Hwy. 95 for 18 miles and turn left on Succor Creek Rd. and drive northwest for 10 miles. Turn left on Leslie Gulch Rd. and follow this down into Leslie Gulch for 14 miles on a well-maintained gravel road.

GPS Coordinates: 43.3118° N, 117.3153° W

Did You Know? The Gulch was originally named Dugout, but it was renamed for Hiram Leslie, a local rancher who was struck by lightning in the canyon in 1882.

Journal:

Date(s) Visited:

Weather conditions:

Who you were with:

Nature observations:

Special memories:

Toketee Falls

One of Oregon's most famous falls, Toketee, is named for the Chinook word meaning "pretty" or "graceful" and is known for the elegant basalt formation that frames its two-stage 120-foot drop.

The trail out to the falls is less than one mile roundtrip and is recommended for all ages. If you want to get a bit closer to the falls, it is easy enough to shimmy through the fencing and work your way down. Wear proper footwear, but the rest of the way down is not too challenging as long as you take your time.

Best time to visit: The trail to the Falls is open year-round. Parking is tight so avoid the weekends.

Pass/Permit/Fees: Entry is free.

Closest city or town: Roseburg

How to get there: From Roseburg: Head east on OR-138 for 58 miles. Turn north onto Forest Rd. 34/Toketee-Rigdon Rd. Cross the first bridge and follow the signs for parking.

GPS Coordinates: 43.2633° N, 122.4337° W

Did You Know? Due to its reliable water flow on the North Umpqua River, Toketee Falls actually ignores the fluctuation in flow during the summer that affects many of Oregon's falls.

Journal:

Date(s) Visited:

Weather conditions:

Who you were with:

Nature observations:

Special memories:

Valley of the Giants

Located in Northwest Oregon, this incredible forest preserve is home to some of Oregon's largest Douglas Firs and Western Hemlock trees, many of which approach five hundred years in age.

An easy 1.4-mile hiking trail leads you to walk through these massive plants and, though the elevation gain is less than 690 feet, there are occasional steep sections where you will want to watch your step and be mindful of roots.

Best time to visit: You'll want to visit December-July, as it's closed the rest of the year for fire season. Aim for weekends since there is often logging activity in the area.

Pass/Permit/Fees: Entry is free.

Closest city or town: Falls City

How to get there: The drive to the trailhead should be researched before embarking, as it's an adventure in itself. Consult with the Bureau of Land Management for directions before departing. Allow at least 90 minutes to travel in each direction.

GPS Coordinates: 44.9399° N, 123.7137° W

Did You Know? "Big Guy" was one of the Valley's most famous trees. Though he was blown down in a windstorm in 1981, the 230-foot-tall tree was thought to be over six hundred years old and the second largest Douglas Fir standing in Oregon.

Journal:

Date(s) Visited:

Weather conditions:

Who you were with:

Nature observations:

Special memories:

Newberry National Volcanic Monument Big Obsidian Flow

This lava flow located in the Newberry Caldera looks nearly identical to when it first cooled after erupting from a magma chamber at a temperature of 1,600ºF. A trail with several interpretive signs details the history and geology of the flow. The trail is a loop that extends a bit longer than half a mile, and is mostly flat and easy, but it's important to be extremely careful since the trail is surrounded by volcanic glass. Wear closed-toed shoes, stay on the trail, take it easy, and everything should be fine!

If you're looking to sit and learn, rangers give talks about Oregon's volcanic history and the national monument throughout the summer at the amphitheater.

Best time to visit: Aim for June-October; seasonal weather conditions can often close this area.

Pass/Permit/Fees: There is a $5 day-use parking fee.

Closest city or town: Bend

How to get there: From Bend: Head south for 24 miles on Hwy. 97, then head east for 15 miles on County Rd. 21, following the signs for the trailhead.

GPS Coordinates: 43.6957° N, 121.2345° W

Did You Know? At a mere 1,300 years old, the Big Obsidian Lava Flow is actually the youngest in Oregon, a reminder that much of Oregon remains actively volcanic.

Journal:

Date(s) Visited:

Weather conditions:

Who you were with:

Nature observations:

Special memories:

Koosah Falls

Koosah means "shining" in Chinook, and this seventy-foot drop along the twenty-six-mile-long McKenzie River Trail lives up to its name.

The Koosah Falls trail loops out to Sahalie Falls and back, so it's two waterfalls per hike. It's only 2.8 miles total, so this is a great hike for beginning hikers or families with children. Keep an eye out along the trail for viewpoints of the McKenzie River.

This is a great area for camping as well, with a few campgrounds just on the edge of the trail.

Best time to visit: Trying to get winter access can be tricky and downright dangerous. Aim for April-October to avoid any snowfall and aim for weekdays since parking is limited.

Pass/Permit/Fees: Entry is free.

Closest city or town: McKenzie Bridge

How to get there: From McKenzie Bridge: Head east on Hwy. 126 to Carmen Reservoir. Just north of the turnoff to Carmen Reservoir, turn left at the Ice Cap Campground/Koosah Falls sign.

GPS Coordinates: 44.3440° N, 122.0006° W

Did You Know? Sahalie Falls, which connects with Koosah Falls, was featured in the Disney movie *Homeward Bound*.

Journal:

Date(s) Visited:

Weather conditions:

Who you were with:

Nature observations:

Special memories:

Tamanawas Falls

Tamanawas Falls flows in a true curtain of water during the right time of year, thundering over a 110-foot lava cliff into a deep pool.

Hiking out to the falls is 3.4 miles on an out-and-back trail that follows Cold Spring Creek and is rated moderate. As you pass through the forest, keep your eyes peeled for native plants like fairy slipper orchids and western wood anemone.

Tamanawas Falls is also close to several campgrounds in case you're wanting to make a day of it.

Best time to visit: The trailhead is open from May to October. This is a good hike for summer due to the density of the forest and the mist from the falls.

Pass/Permit/Fees: There is a $5 day-use parking fee.

Closest city or town: Hood River

How to get there: From Hood River: Head south on Hwy. 35 for 25 miles to the Pollallie Trailhead (north access) If you continue on Hwy. 35 for five more miles, you reach the Tamanawas Falls trailhead (south access) with a parking area on the west side of the highway.

GPS Coordinates: 45.3972° N, 121.5716° W

Did You Know? Sure-footed climbers can access a dry cave from the trail as well, but it is recommended to bring a rain jacket!

Journal:

Date(s) Visited:

Weather conditions:

Who you were with:

Nature observations:

Special memories:

Latourell Falls

One of the multitudes of waterfalls in the Columbia River Gorge in Oregon — Latourell Falls — manages to stand out regardless. While most of the area's waterfalls tumble down to some degree, Latourell Falls is a straight 249-foot drop over its basalt cliff.

The Lower Falls can be seen driving by on the Historic Columbia River Highway and visitors can take a short walk to a viewing platform, but there is a 2.1-mile trail that leads to the waterfall itself. The hike is rated easy-to-moderate and there is a picnic area for reservation for those who would rather sit and enjoy the view.

Best time to visit: Aim for late spring, when the snow has thawed and the waterfall is at its heaviest.

Pass/Permit/Fees: Entry is free.

Closest city or town: Portland

How to get there: From Portland: Head east on I-84 for 30 miles and take Exit 28 to Bridal Veil. Follow signs on the Historic Columbia River Hwy. for three miles for Latourell Falls.

GPS Coordinates: 45.5370° N, 122.2178° W

Did You Know? Latourell Falls is part of George W. Joseph State Natural Area, named for the Oregon family who donated the land to the state in the 1930s and 40s.

Journal:

Date(s) Visited:

Weather conditions:

Who you were with:

Nature observations:

Special memories:

Tumalo Falls

Tumalo Falls may seem little with a 97-foot drop, but this popular waterfall packs a lot of punch. With an area for picnicking and several trails for hiking and mountain biking, there's a lot to do in this section of Deschutes National Forest.

The hike is moderate and features a few add-ons if you're craving a longer jaunt, but the hike to the waterfall viewing platform is only one-quarter mile. Hiking another 1.25 miles leads to Middle Tumalo Falls, a 65-foot two-tiered cascade.

Best time to visit: The trail can be hiked year-round, but the access road closes in the winter. Wait for the snow to melt and visit around the end of spring for a beautiful waterfall and aim for a weekday or early morning to avoid the crowds at this popular site.

Pass/Permit/Fees: There is a $5 day-use parking fee.

Closest city or town: Bend

How to get there: From Bend: Head west on Skyliner's Rd. (4601) for 12 miles, then head west for three miles on Forest Rd. 4603. Follow the signs for the trailhead and parking lot.

GPS Coordinates: 44.0340° N, 121.5669° W

Did You Know? Tumalo Creek is twenty miles long and provides water for farmland and drinking water for the city of Bend.

Journal:

Date(s) Visited:

Weather conditions:

Who you were with:

Nature observations:

Special memories:

Other Places

Place: _____

Date(s) visited:

Weather conditions:

Who you were with:

Nature observations:

Special memories:

Place: _____

Date(s) visited:

Weather conditions:

Who you were with:

Nature observations:

Special memories:

Place: _____

Date(s) visited:

Weather conditions:

Who you were with:

Nature observations:

Special memories:

Place: _____

Date(s) visited:

Weather conditions:

Who you were with:

Nature observations:

Special memories:

Place: _____

Date(s) visited:

Weather conditions:

Who you were with:

Nature observations:

Special memories:

Place: _____

Date(s) visited:

Weather conditions:

Who you were with:

Nature observations:

Special memories:

Place: _____

Date(s) visited:

Weather conditions:

Who you were with:

Nature observations:

Special memories:

Place: _____

Date(s) visited:

Weather conditions:

Who you were with:

Nature observations:

Special memories:

Place: _____

Date(s) visited:

Weather conditions:

Who you were with:

Nature observations:

Special memories:

Place: _____

Date(s) visited:

Weather conditions:

Who you were with:

Nature observations:

Special memories:

Credit the Incredible Photographers:

Old Fort Road Gravity Hill
https://www.atlasobscura.com/places/gravity-hill
"okn0tok. (2019). Old Fort Road Gravity Hill. https://www.atlasobscura.com/places/gravity-hill. Atlas Obscura. https://www.atlasobscura.com/places/gravity-hill."

Lava River Cave
https://search.creativecommons.org/photos/2e0418d6-6df2-46a5-8f39-82d71c03f0db
"Lava River Cave" by Coconino NF Photography is marked under CC PDM 1.0. To view the terms, visit https://creativecommons.org/publicdomain/mark/1.0/

Haystack Rock
https://search.creativecommons.org/photos/a0f3324f-19b4-48f6-aaaf-06389d17c789
"Haystack Rock - Cannon Beach, Oregon" by Dougtone is licensed with CC BY-SA 2.0. To view a copy of this license, visit https://creativecommons.org/licenses/by-sa/2.0/

Multnomah Falls
https://search.creativecommons.org/photos/3ccd1cea-2714-42e0-8a51-e44125ed29e8
"Multnomah Falls" by LukeDetwiler is licensed with CC BY 2.0. To view a copy of this license, visit https://creativecommons.org/licenses/by/2.0/

Neahkahnie Mountain
https://search.creativecommons.org/photos/12cc732a-3d8a-4ad4-a7d7-4e5a32b4768e
"Neahkahnie mountain hike" by Jeff Alworth is licensed with CC BY 2.0. To view a copy of this license, visit https://creativecommons.org/licenses/by/2.0/

Crack in the Ground
https://search.creativecommons.org/photos/92c4c6d6-a948-42df-834a-590407a6522a
"Crack in the Ground" by BLM Oregon & Washington is licensed with CC BY 2.0. To view a copy of this license, visit https://creativecommons.org/licenses/by/2.0/

Mount Thielsen Fulgurites
https://search.creativecommons.org/photos/be7eeb16-eb50-4f0f-8485-b56a12db6bce
"Mount Thielson, As Seen from South Rim of Crater Lake National Park, Oregon" by Ken Lund is licensed with CC BY-SA 2.0. To view a copy of this license, visit https://creativecommons.org/licenses/by-sa/2.0/

Mt. Hood
https://search.creativecommons.org/photos/1415a087-af8e-4abf-b33d-bf8061a3596d
"Nature - Mt Hood, Oregon" by Trodel is licensed with CC BY-SA 2.0. To view a copy of this license, visit https://creativecommons.org/licenses/by-sa/2.0/

Hells Canyon
https://search.creativecommons.org/photos/ff2a2c7e-c220-4a8f-9194-60fb85a4df2d
"Hell's Canyon, Oregon" by Bonnie Moreland (free images) is marked under CC PDM 1.0. To view the terms, visit https://creativecommons.org/publicdomain/mark/1.0/

Alvord Desert
https://search.creativecommons.org/photos/768201f5-2c81-4129-af17-351bf6d916a4

Waldo Lake
https://search.creativecommons.org/photos/0fe3cd5a-522b-4dd8-8c6f-4204992b75ce
"North Shore, Waldo Lake, Oregon" by Bonnie Moreland (free images) is marked under CC PDM 1.0.
To view the terms, visit https://creativecommons.org/publicdomain/mark/1.0/

Table Rock
https://search.creativecommons.org/photos/633ec934-9111-43e1-a92c-50352c8b51b4
"Upper Table Rock" by BLM Oregon & Washington is licensed with CC BY 2.0. To view a copy of this
license, visit https://creativecommons.org/licenses/by/2.0/

Mount McLoughlin
https://search.creativecommons.org/photos/534cbe1a-ccd4-40a3-a947-987b77385dd5
"Mount McLoughlin From Brown Mountain" by ex_magician is licensed with CC BY 2.0. To view a copy
of this license, visit https://creativecommons.org/licenses/by/2.0/

Umpqua National Forest
https://search.creativecommons.org/photos/7dbab62d-b5d7-4eb6-9adb-be97daed251f
"Lake and Forest, Umpqua National Forest-2.jpg" by Forest Service Pacific Northwest Region is
marked under CC PDM 1.0. To view the terms, visit
https://creativecommons.org/publicdomain/mark/1.0/

Cape Meares
https://search.creativecommons.org/photos/8bb1ce0f-87c8-4467-af71-fc612ee02082
"Cape Meares" by USFWS Headquarters is licensed with CC BY 2.0. To view a copy of this license, visit
https://creativecommons.org/licenses/by/2.0/

Devil's Churn
https://search.creativecommons.org/photos/673711aa-a356-4af0-929c-7fe9c9e60cf3
"Devils Churn" by Kirt Edblom is licensed with CC BY-SA 2.0. To view a copy of this license, visit
https://creativecommons.org/licenses/by-sa/2.0/

Arnold Ice Cave
https://search.creativecommons.org/photos/99e4aebe-9e9b-40ce-b8f3-ece0b730d497
"Arnold Ice Cave near Bend, Oregon" by Dan Nevill is licensed with CC BY 2.0. To view a copy of this
license, visit https://creativecommons.org/licenses/by/2.0/

Natural Bridges Cove
https://search.creativecommons.org/photos/73291505-8976-4e83-b7af-d2e144be3880
"Natural Bridges Cove - Boardman State Park, Oregon" by Rick McCharles is licensed with CC BY 2.0.
To view a copy of this license, visit https://creativecommons.org/licenses/by/2.0/

Elowah Falls
https://search.creativecommons.org/photos/ecddc8c6-bd06-4200-a140-70550c7c40c2
"Elowah Falls" by Ian Sane is licensed with CC BY 2.0. To view a copy of this license, visit
https://creativecommons.org/licenses/by/2.0/

Salt Creek Falls
https://search.creativecommons.org/photos/529268bb-93c5-47bd-86ac-3d2b7aaa0bdb

Made in the USA
Coppell, TX
01 October 2021

63274730R00075